"What chess taught me"
Or

The logic of when systems get complicated

zerreit

2021

Naucalpan, Edo de México, México

"What chess taught me" Or

The logic of when systems get complicated

Second Edition

zerreit

To order additional copies of this book, contact:
Palibrio
1663 Liberty Drive, Suite 200
Bloomington, IN 47403
Toll Free from the U.S.A 877.407.5847
Toll Free from Mexico 01.800.288.2243
Toll Free from Spain 900.866.949
From other International locations +1.812.671.9757
Fax: 01.812.355.1576
orders@palibrio.com
831251

Dedicated to my son:
Ing. Francisco Quiroz Collazo

Contents

I specially thanks to
Josefina Margarita Collazo Ramírez
his great help, not only in the
corrections, but in many of the
ideas that allowed me to build
this book.

Read me 1ST

Dear reader:

This small book aims to introduce you to the art of thinking that a good chess player has. He who achieves through the management of his resources the triumph or the defeat. The first one will give you the satisfaction of having won, the second one the impetus to start over again.

Probably, this is the first chess book, which is not dedicated to chess players, for its reading it does not even need the knowledge of how to move the pieces on the board of the so-called science game. Although I only wish that my friends, both chess players from all the clubs I have visited, as well as simple "chess players of life" find in this book, the projection into their lives that chess grants.

It is dedicated to all those who wish to learn to make an analysis of their present, without contaminating it with their past, and so they can use it for the benefit of the construction of their future.

To all those who despite the pain of having lost, are willing to "put the pieces back together" and start again a new experience wishing you win this time.

Introduction

Quite a long time, - while I was organizing my mind, I keep on saying phrases in conversations with my friends. When they asked me where I had gotten this or that concept:

Chess taught me that!

So, I acquire debt for miself for one day attempting these essays. Chess is first and foremost a model of strategy, and it's more than science is a kind of art that we could define as the art that teaches us:

The best use of our resources.

Although, it seems that the very idea of strategy, is more linked to war and therefore to death than to life, thesis whose antithesis I will try to demonstrate.

This is not the case, as:

"Chess is a beautiful model of life".

Chapter I.- Intuitive Strategy or Strategic Intuition?

It was from the war that ancient Greeks invented its name *stratos* = army and *agein* = to lead) and the Dictionary of the Spanish Royal Academy of Language, defines it as:

"The Art of Directing Military Actions"

Or in a figurative sense such as:

"The art or trace to direct some matter."

The strategy has existed since the Greeks baptized it, the essential *sinequa non* condition to be able to be a general and leader of an army.

However, the strategy has been much more than a simple ruse of war made with cunning, and something much more than the simple ability to manage such matter to which the dictionary referred to.

In fact, when the experts who deal with it have attempt to define it, they have not been able to agree.

The range of definitions that have been given to strategy range from:

"The science of the General" to **"the art of making war on the map"** passing through simply and bureaucratically to describe it as **"the coordination of operations to carry out war"**.

They have also tried to look at it as mathematics (meaning formalize it) It was so fashionable that there were people who strive to make formulas and geometric figures to achieve the triumph, forgetting that war is a matter of the mass behavior of men who collide, an essence that escapes the rigidity and precision of all calculations.

It is a question of Complex Systems that sciences like Sociology or Economics, have not been able to formalize up to now.

Perhaps the subtleness of its essence can give us a better idea of what strategy is. The strategy cannot be compared to simply its logistics (word that derived from the French: *logistique* = placement which gives only an idea of an accommodation).

To compare the strategy to bare logistics would be as foolish as to compare the great pleasure of playing chess to the simple fact of placing the pieces on the board. This in fact constitutes a first degree of inventory according to the theory of inventory. The bureaucrats reduce strategy to this thought.

May be, we will understand strategy better, if we consider that unlike other arts that combine in their goals, beauty, harmony, proportion, symmetry, and many other properties that the human spirit enjoys, the strategy has one goal: victory. Its main problem is the achievement of victory*.

In strategy, making a well-done plan to achieve a goal is not simply an prosaic task (as Rubió would call it, in his Dictionary of Military Sciences); making up a plan that

---

* Unlike the sciences, that pursue a scientific truth that will never reach, and propose their theories, which are no doubt useful is terms of truth are like the beautiful miniskirts.

4

is acceptable already offers a difficulty to the person who tries it. Being able to choose the best possible plan is already a task that can only be performed by a clear and select intelligence. But being able to identify the objectives, relativity its value every time, combine the problems and resources and finally being able to carry it out successfully:

**This can only be achieved
by the strategist!**

It occurs to me that a good definition for strategy could be found in the Royal Spanish Academy of Language Dictionary, in the definition it gives us for art. If we simply change the word "something" for "triumph" it would make sense.

**"Strategy is the virtue, the willingness
or industry to achieve triumph."**

Perhaps that is why the essence of life, both in biology and in our daily life, is the permanent struggle in which:

Each triumph only serves to face a new challenge.

This is the reason why chess is like strategy. In this, more than in any other art, success depends essentially on the use we make of our resources, on our ability to identified them, to face them, to our problem - in which **every problem is a** negative **resource**- to use them in the most intelligent way, to be careful not to destroy them when using them, and to be sure multiply them.

That is why the great strategists of humanity have only revealed their genius during the war, when the victory hangs in the subtlest mistake. The victory is only achieved by using the right resource in the right place, always at the right time. And this happens to every resource!

Only conditions like the ones that caused the Mexican Revolution were able to generate a Pancho Villa or an Emiliano Zapata; or the situation of France in the XVIII Century, produced a Napoleon and an turn the problems that Wellington.

Chapter II.- Problems vs Resources and Tom Thumb Tactic

Chess would not have the great complication that delights us, unless for conjugation of resources. They depend on their situations on the board (meaning space) and in each of their moves (meaning time), generate in turn new problems, which must be faced with resources.

Resources that are modified with a single move from the opponent and therefore what it was a resource in the previous move, might no longer be, just as it happens in real life.

This reminds me Karl Popper's words. The English philosopher in a scientific session about reductionism, said:

"We live in a world in which novelty springs up, in a world that confronts us with some problems that if we solve them, we will only fall into greater problem and a different ssituation that cannot be reduced even to the immediate situation before."

Chapter III.- Strategic Intuition or Intuitive Strategy

In chess and strategy, as in poetry, arts, and sciences, it is not enough to have a great intelligence, but a special creativity. A characteristic that distinguishes geniuses from chess, art, and science.

In addition, it's necessary a certain intuition that chess players have called: **the chess sense.** Later, we will demonstrate this sense is the best example of "heuristic" knowledge. The knowledge that is there (translation from Greek), and that allowed experts in artificial intelligence to develop expert systems[*].

---

[*] Perhaps the best model of computational architecture of these expert systems is the design of the new computer programs for contemporary chess that use different families (meaning experts). Programs that use huge memories in the opening, copied strategies in the middle game, and algorithms

And of course, as in poetry, arts and sciences, the special taste of the good chess player is the **pleasure of solving a problem**.

The reasons why we can say, that as a model of strategy chess, is rather a model of a **"Little prince science"**, a **"discreet resourcelogy"** or well a **"limited resourcelogy" in** which the space has been diminished (meaning discretized) to sixty-four squares (something that had not been required in the same cellular automata[**]), and the time (meaning limited) has been limited to making a single decision each chess move. and the time (meaning limited) has been limited to making a single decision each play.

---

with a tremendous force that have swept the entire scope of possible endings.

[**] Mathematical tool that uses grids and a discrete number of instructions to solve problems.

Since, before the middle game, the moves seem infinite and perhaps "*quasi*" are, after the middle game the chances are reduced with the same logarithmic slope and in the end decrease, without turning the end of the game less interesting or tedious. If we study many chess games, we will see that although there is no rule in its regulations that limits the game of exceeding a certain number of moves, it is rare to find a game with more than a hundred moves. This is for the simple unwritten reason that from the opening it is obligatory to reach the middle game which leads to the end. Although a game can become endless and be drawn, it can only be lost or won.

And similar to life, which generates very large amounts with the combination a few numbers, in chess, with the combination of a few elements (a few numbers), an almost infinite number of situations and problems arise, which make this game, remain forever young.

As any system of knowledge based on rules, a regulation (meaning restrictions) was put to it. The French mathematician H. Pathé would say:

"We have a new form of the chicken-and-egg paradox":

"What was first the constraints that generate a language, or the language generated the restrictions?"

A group of constraints generates a grammar. Nowadays, mathematicians have taken the idea of grammar from a set of spelling rules to be the rules of a system that supports a theory.

Chess without being a cellular automaton generates a grammar and a language. Chess without being mathematical, like life -and like any theory- obeys a logic in which the propositions instead of being used to build the tables of truth that help us to value things without being true or false. It will only lead us to assess if the moves (meaning propositions), were the correct ones to achieve the triumph.

Reasons why chess is also a model and luckily an amazingly simple one, of a new science as it originates itself from observation and experimentation within its scope.

It is a model that would be responsible for studying the best use of resources. This science, which is in fact the Little Thumbling of the sciences, requires for its conformation of only four postulates.

They become questions that constitute the scheme of thought of the chess player, who inadvertently only uses the system of that universal logic, which we have suggested to call "Logic of When Systems Get Complicated"

Chapter IV.-The Logic of When Systems Get Complicated

The system that gets the most complicated for us is our very life.

The thesis contained in this writing, is that chess can teach us to analyze a little our life, since at the end of the day: Chess is a particularly good model of the logic of when systems get complicated.

The complicated systems can be defined as sets, where their elements interact with each other, in such a way that: The system is different from the sum of its parts. A philosophical principle that J.C. Smuts precursor of systemic thinking called holistic in 1926 says: *"All reality is composed of an organized whole."*

Recently, the antithesis of this feature, the holistic, has been called: "Principle of superposition". It is used by experts in computerized biological simulation (which has boastfully been called *artificial life)* They find that systems that share behaviors similar to life, or with certain characteristics of biological systems, have as their main characteristic the "non-linearity" characterized by not complying with this principle of superposition that makes in linear systems, that the analysis of each of its parts in independent form allows the reconstruction of the system and its behaviors.

Nonlinear systems as life, in which it is not possible to predict behaviors, even though they are ruled by restrictions (a principle that our third world statesmen seem to ignore), do not follow the principle of superposition. So, in these systems the integration of their different components generates unexpected behavior which are the interest of programmers who are interested in the "artificial life.

When systems get complicated, problems among the members of the system occur, which is none other than: The difference between a desired situation and a situation achieved.

And to solve these problems the chess player generates resources, which are not only the presence of his pieces on the board but rather how he uses them. A well-known principle of every chess player is:

The pieces are worth the place they occupy on the board.

This principle of chess matches with the fundamental principle of strategy, which is the concentration of forces, a principle that the old generals expressed by saying:

"An army must disperse to survive and concentrate on fighting."

This principle indicates the importance of avoiding the disintegration of efforts, a lack in which one frequently incur in chess as in life by not estimating the magnitude of a problem. The great Napoleon said about it:

"You're never strong enough in a battle. Every troop unit must turn to the noise of combat."

Principle of concentration of resources, which for Bonaparte was not only was operative in the offensive, as in another of his texts he expresses:

"... [..]. The aggressive and active, maneuvering defense could also have amazing results if in exchange of its inferiority it had the ability to be at the right time at the right place, turning the defense into a set of intelligent counterattacks."

This situation makes the chess players think of the rebirth of the openings in chess such as the recently put into fashion Meztel Defense by the British champion of the seventies.

This concentration of forces in chess is a perfect example that the best use of the pieces on the board is not just pile them in one place, but to achieve their proper location so that they have combined and potential effect (meaning optimize them).

Every player knows that a horse located on a corner has, up to two moves. When it is on the edge of the board and away from the corner it has up to four moves. But when a horse is in the center it can have eight moves. Therefore, a player learns from the beginning to place his pieces in the center.

Chapter V.-Scientific Truth vs Chess Truth

Truth in chess as in strategy is the **only truth that demonstrates itself**. It does not need to be accepted by a committee of experts as science does. Truth in chess is either happy or painful because unlike truth in science, fashion or culture are nothing but:

Propositions that have not been proven false and are accepted by a committee of experts

The truth of chess does not require expert judgment to acquire that axiological characteristic born of a majority, a market motivation, or a democracy.

Its efficiency is obvious any time since, a language comes from the moves (meaning propositions) that the rules of chess allow (what current experts in rule-based knowledge systems will call its **grammar)**

The logic language of when systems get complicated.

A language that chess players feel. What is better than their sepulchral silence in which the humming of their neurons is almost heard, silence only broken by the word check!

Language of propositions, that unlike other languages that have the logic of predicates as basis, this time it is not important if the propositions are true or false.

In this kind of language, there are no tables of truth that describe the result as false or true.

In this language, as in life, the qualifier is the efficiency of the system. The efficiency that the words of the wise Napoleonic judgment had already predicted:

"Winning a lost cause, is not winning".

In chess as in life the result is not only not continuous, but also discrete, the result is only one. Chess is a war where battles are unimportant, the important thing is the end. And no chess player would consider as triumph the accumulation of pieces from which he is faring badly.

Chapter VI.-What Chess Advised Me

As in chess the result of the proposition we make depends on the next move (meaning the immediate future of the system). But once the immediate future of the system becomes present, the chess player can no longer regret what is now his past, no matters how immediate this past may seem to him.

Perhaps the first great lesson that chess gives us: is that the chess player, like the man, only has his present time to make his game.

We have said that chess seen as *the Little Science for resources studing* or, as a little prince science is only composed of four laws that used as rules give us the framework to generate a behavior But we can turn them into questions, and by doing so they allow us to analyze any complicated system and quite possibly:

The most interesting, complex and complicated system, for us, our very life.

But curiously our little science, shows us that the difficulties of our daily life, for the purposes of this analysis, are similar to the difficulties of the function of a factory, a bank, an office, a hospital, a university or polytechnic institute. And that in a very wise are the same questions followed by Mother Nature in her work. These questions are:

I.- Do I know my resources?
II.- Knowing them I use them?
III.- When using them: do I take care of not destroying them?

IV.- Do I produce new resources?

Questions that in the form of advice, could be the best lesson that Mother Nature can teach to her creatures.

Chapter VII.- Chess, Metaphor of life, in Poetry.

Chess, from its earliest years, has been an exciting topic that has inspired to many poets and writers throughout the world.

The chessboard as a confrontation stage of passions, meeting of minds, space of loves and heartbreaks. And the pieces symbolizing the people, in their life, their fight, his death.

Within the most beautiful metaphors, one that shows a human existence predetermined and directed by an entity superior, a God, is the one who has given us by Jorge Luis Borges:

In their solemn corner, the players move
The slow pieces. The board detains them

Until the dawn in its severe world
In which two colors hate each other.

Within the forms irradiate magic
Strictness: Homeric rook, swift
Knight, armed queen, hintermost king,
Oblique bishop and aggressor pawns.

Once the players have finally left,
Once time has devoured them,
Surely the ritual will not have ended.

In the orient this very war flared up
Whose amphitheater today
is the earth entire.
Like the other, this game is infinite.

Weakling king slanting bishop, relentless
Queen, direct rook and cunning pawn
Seek and wage their armed battle
Across the black and white of the field.

They know not that the players notorious
Hand governs their destiny,
They know not that a rigor adamantine
Subjects their will and rules their day.

The player also is a prisoner
(The saying is Omars) of another board
Of black nights and of white days.
God moves the player, and he, the piece.
Which god behind God begets the plot
Of dust and time and
dream and agonies?

In his poem Borges clarifies that a certain
sentence is not of his invention but of the
persian astronomer, mathematician and
poet of the 10th century, Omar-alKhayyam,
that in one of his poems mentioned chess:

**Because this life is not
-how to prove you I hope-,
more than a fuzzy board**

of complicated chess.
The white squares: the days the
black squares: the nights...

And before the board, destiny
act there with men,
as with moving parts
at his whim without order...
And one after another to the case
Go. Out of nowhere without a name.

"Chess is a Touchstone for intelligence"

Rosario Castellanos writer, journalist and Mexican diplomat, considered one of the most important Mexican literates of the twentieth century, in his poem denominated "Chess", uses chess as a metaphor to relationships; taking friendships to another level, making boundaries between each other, and how to score the others heart. This poem use

the steps of chess to explain: how human
relationship evolve:

Because we were friends and
sometimes loved each other,
perhaps to add one more tie
to the many that already bound us,
we decided to play games of the mind.

We set up a board between us:
equally divided into pieces, values,
and possible moves.
We learned the rules,
we swore to respect them,
and the match began.

We've been sitting here for
centuries, meditating
ferociously
how to deal the one last
blow that will finally
annihilate the other one forever.

Capítulo VIII.- Chess in Literature

Chess has caught the attention of scholars, scientist, writers and men of thought, who have leaning into his study from the angles that offer their sociological significance and its historical meaning.

In his work **Goetz von Berlichingen** mercenary of the 16th century, whose autobiography inspired **Goethe** to write his well-known tragedy Götz von Berlichingen (first performed in 1773), puts in mouth of one of the protagonists, the phrase that has become famous:

Cry of freedom!

---

*In which Götz appears as one of the last feudal lords, absorbed by imperial centralism, and therefore as a character suitable for painting heroically falling with the final. Shortly afterwards Schiller would take, with greater conviction, the same theme as the axis of almost all his works.

Julio Ganzo in his **"History of Chess"** mentions that the great writer was not very affective of chess, although it was his mother, a woman who caused one of his admirers wrote: *"God should having created all men in the image of her"*, the lady gathered four passions, make lace, play the harpsichord, read and play chess.

Which reminds me of a tip from Antonio Quiroz: "Don't you get old, old if you don't have three things:
1.-A great emotion
2.-A great illusion Y
3.-A vice and of these I recommend you to Chess.

Miguel de Cervantes Saavedra, put in his inmortal Don Quixote de la Mancha the folowing:

"Brave comparison," said Sancho, although not so new that I have not heard many and various times, such as that of the game of aiedrez, that while the game lasts each piece remains his particular job, and in the end of I play they all mix, gather and shuffle, and they find them in a bag, which is how to find life in the grave".

Juan Huarte de San Juan, physician and philosopher Spanish of the S XVI, in his book **Exam of Ingenios para las Ciencias**, says:

"And it was the mystery that the master had great understanding, with which reached the delicacies of Escoto and of Saint Thomas, and was lacking that difference of imaginative with who plays chess, and the waiter

*had understanding and memory
and very delicate imagination".*

Mateo Alemán y de Nero, Sevillian writer of the Spanish Golden Age, in his novel picaresque Guzmán de Alfarache says:

*"He took over the business, and
started from that point to start
the game, giving traces like the one
proposes to give a mate in chess to so
many sets in the designated house."*

Saint Teresa of Jesus[*] on her *"Camino de perfection"* tells us:

*"Well, believe that who does not know
arrange the pieces in the game of*

---

[*] Proclaimed a doctor of the Catholic Church in 1970 and one of the great teachers of the spiritual life of the Church.

the chess, which will taste bad to play, and if not. He knows how to check, he will not know how to mate. You will have to rebuke me, because I'm talking about gambling, not having in this house, not even having: here you will see the Mother, who gave you God, that even this vanity knew; more They say it is legal sometimes. And how it will be lawful for us this way to play, and how quickly, if much we use, we will kill this King divine, that we will not be able to leave the hands or want. The lady is the one who war can make you in this game, and all the other pieces help."

Francisco de Quevedo in his: "Casa crazy about love", he mentions the game science: "This one went to all parties at fall in love, making the days of work, and that one was home at home, as a chess piece, never being able to take a lady."

Marie de Rabutin-Chantal, Marchioness of Sévigné, French writer of the 16th century. In his Epistolary she refers:

"This gentleman has told me that sometimes you play chess: I'm crazy about this game; I would give a lot of money for know it, only that as my son or like you. It is the most beautiful and the most rational of all games; chance it does not intervene in it; one is censored and it is applauded; you have happiness in head. And I assure you that I will be very ashamed and very humiliated, if I do not at least reach a medium force. In Pomponne, during the last wretched trip. What did I do there, everyone played chess: men, women, children..."

Santiago Ramón y Cajal Spanish physician, Nobel Prize in Medicine in 1906 for discover the mechanisms that govern morphology and connective processes of neurons, in his posthumous work *"Memories of my life"* he tells us:

"Excused is to say that I acquired how many books of the aristocratic recess came into my hands and I even fell into the innocence to send to artwork foreign problem solutions. Carried away by the growing passion, my dreams were interrupted by dreams and nightmares, in which they armed frenzied zarabanda pawns, knights, queens and bishops."

Already in the 20th century Stefan Zweig, in his novel *"A Game Of Chess"* presents the clash of two antagonistic natures, in words of his character Mirko Czentovicz:

"It is a thought that does not lead to nowhere, a mathematics that does not establishes nothing, an art that does not leave behind any work, an architecture without matter; and despite this chess has shown be more durable, in its own way, tan books or any other kind of monument. This unique game belongs to all peoples and at all times, and no one you can know about him, what divinity gave her down to earth to kill boredom, sharpen the spirit and stimulate the soul.

Chapter IX Chess in the Pedagogy

*«I don't teach my students, I just
I provide the conditions
in which they can learn «.*
                        Albert Einstein.

According to Plato:

*"Education consists of guiding
the intelligence towards the true
object of knowledge, which is the
understanding of idea of the Good"*

And according to him:

*"To awaken intelligence is a prioritery
necessary to develop the capacities
and control irrational desires".*

Plato sought, through education, to
liberate the soul of the body that held

him prisoner. In his brilliant mind he was already advancing in more than XXV Centuries to modern Philosophy of the mind.

The idea of the usefulness of chess in pedagogy, I was already in the USA since the very birth of this nation in the Century XVIII; as in one of his writings **Benjamin Franklin,** considered one of the Founding Fathers of the United States from North America proves it:

"Chess is not just frivolous fun,
but his practice develops several
very valuable mental qualities in life
normal, since life is frequently a kind
of chess game, where we need to
have a vision of the future, weigh
the consequences of our acts, take
responsibility for themselves, always
have one part -, measure risks

well an overview of the situation or the board - and not only and —And not only and dangers, and scrupulously respect the rules".

It is well known The rusian people's love and predilection for chess, from the time of the tsars. They were the first to do of him a profession, treat him almost like a sport of the mind, create your schools and make Russia the first power world chess.

But what happened in 1966 when the champion world at that time, Garri Kasparov was defeated by the program computer program named **Deep Blue**, milestone unexpected in the chess world that demonstrate, as Fermín Revueltas, mexican mathematician and chess player said:

"When playing chess became like play chess with God"

This sucess not only changed the way to see the game; this change too algorithmic analysis, statistical posibilities, and psychological requirements, showed that chess requires reflection; needs to as condition sine qua non of the correct care utilization, application from thought to activity performs and concentration, ability of voluntarily isolating themselves from the world exterior and focus exclusively on the action that is performed. Precisely the jauja pedagogical thought, which also made you think that chess practice, would enhance those capabilities.

So in 2011 it was held in Moscow the event *"The teaching of chess in Russia and the rest of the world"* organized by Alexander Kostiev, holder of the Chair of State and Social University Chess of Moscow and Secretary of the Commission World for Schools.

After 3 days of lecturing on the inclusion of chess as a compulsory subject in the schools, agreed to do so by virtue of who concluded that:

"Chess is a powerful instrument for development children's intellectual".

In Spain that in addition to his hobby, love and enthusiasm for chess, inherited everything the patriarchal sentiment for gambling science, which has one of its origins in the Arabian World, his subject was introduced obligatory and on time school.

Even on March 13, 2012, 415 Members of Parliament European many of then spaniards supported the recommendation to introduce chess in the Union Colleges European.

In the 80's, Howard Gardner Harvard University psychologist, in his book "Frames of Mind: The Theory of Multiple Intelligences", stated that chess players largely develop their spatial intelligence, and proposes chess as one of the fields in which they stand out the "prodigies", those people who stand out in a specific field, or one of their intelligences, and they have a performance normal in other areas.

In the years 1973-1974, it was carried out in the Democratic Republic of the Congo, such time the first pedagogical research outside Russia, on the benefits of chess in children and young people: The **"Zaire Chess Experiment"** under the direction of Dr. Albert Frank.

In it, they gave chess classes to 92 students between 16 and 18 years old, and found that chess had a positive influence; improved reasoning, intelligence, creativity, quick planning, visión fifty spatial and improved understanding of geometry.

In 1974 to 1976 at the University of Luvaina in Belgium, Professor Johan Christaen, carried out a study in which they used to 40 children with a mean age of 10.6 years, randomly divided into a couple of groups. One of the groups was given 42 hours chess classes and were provided with the book "Chess for young people", shortly after, The 2 groups were given tests cognitive development and outcomes can be summarized with the same words of their conclusions:

"We have scientific bases that reaffirm what we already knew: chess makes children smarter".

For those same years, not just the Old Continent, but Latin America, including Cuba, separately discovered the advantages of teaching chess.

In 1982 the former Minister of Education of the United States Terrel Bell, stated in his book "Excellence" that:

«One of the best and most fun ways to develop your son's intelligence was teaching him to play chess."

Shortly after chess was introduced in schools in the United States, focusing on the Harlem district.

The **NYCHESS Program** (program of chess in New York schools), showed that chess instills the sense self-confidence and self-esteem, improves rational thinking and increases cognitive skills, especially in mathematics and language, as well as their communication skills by 17.3% of students who participated with regularity in chess classes, in compared to only 4.56% of children control who did not take part.

In the years 1988 and 1989 in Venezuela, Edelmira García de la Rosa, promoted the Project "Learning to think", in which investigated whether chess could be used in the development of children's intelligence. After a year of studies, she found than chess, increased the Intellectual Coefficient, both in boys and girls. And given the success of this project, it was applied in all the schools in this country.

In 1992 Dr. Stuart Margulies published his article ***The Effect of Chess on Reading Scores***: mentions among his observations, a correlation between playing chess and a increased reading comprehension. In his words: *«The students who learned to play chess enjoyed a raise significant in their reading ability»*

In 1995 UNESCO officially recommended to its member countries, the incorporation of chess as a subject educational, both in primary education as secondary; what took place of different ways: in some countries like Venezuela or Colombia chess forms mandatory part of the curriculum of students; while others include as an optional subject.

After the 90s, they have been conducted numerous studies that would be long list in this libello, with results quite similar. For whoever would like to go Deep into the subject, I recommended the publication **"Teaching mathematics**

with chess resources", by Joaquín Gairín Sallán and Joaquín Fernández-Friend of the Autonomous University of Barcelona.

Children who play chess show significant improvement in areas as important as spatial thinking, numerical and analytical skills, verbal communication, and even artistic imagination.

But: **how does it specifically help chess to children and young people?**

In the years 2020 and 2021, Dr. Telmo Pereira and his group from the Polytechnic Institutem of Coimbra in Portugal and the Universities of Cáceres and Extremadura in Spain. In their paper: **"Neurophysiological and autonomic responses of high and low level chess players during difficult and easy chess endgames"**

They studied and reported a group of 28 chess players divided into two subgroups according to their ELO level (rating system used by the international chess federation):

1.- High level chess players (more than 1600 of ELO score);

and

2.- Low level chess players (ELO less than 1599 of ELO score). Chess players had to complete two easy and two difficult endgames while the electroencephalographic activity and heart rate variability were assessed.

They report in their conclussion that high level chess players exhibit more alpha EEG power spectrums (p-value>0.05) during difficult than during easy chess endgames in the occipital area (O1 and O2 electrodes).

Moreover, high performance players showed a reduced autonomic modulation (p-value>0.05) during the difficult chess endgames which low performance players did not reach.

These results could suggest that high level chess players adapt their neurophysiological response to the task demand, compared the dynamics of the prefrontal cortex of the brain, in players of adolescent and adult chess, during rising level problem solving of difficulty.

Their results indicated that the left cerebral prefrontal cortex, increased its activation with the difficulty of the chess problem.

The cerebral prefrontal cortex, also called **frontal associative cortex** and **magister of the mind,** has been described as the center cognitive function, on which they depend executive functions including making decision, problem solving, also participates in attention, memory, planning, motor control and brain plasticity*

Since the year 2002 Elkhonon Goldberg, neuroscientist from the University of New York in his book "**The Human Brain in era of innovation".** asked in a rigorous way:

What are the brain processes behind of human creativity?

What are they evolutionary roots? How does culture help to shape individual creativity?

---

* Also known as neural plasticity, is the ability of neural networks in the brain to change through growth and reorganization, changes thaat range from individual neuron pathways making new connections, to systematic adjustments like cortical remapping. Somme examples include circuit and network changes that result from learning a new ability, environmental influences, practice, and psychological stress.

Based on the latest discoveries of brain research and its own points of view, unified history, culture and evolution and arrived at an original and provocative understanding of nature of human creativity, the origins of language, nature, and animal cognition.

And showed that the prefrontal cerebral cortex, is found interconnected with other brain regions that allow him to implement the general coordination of the behavior, language and reasoning and problem solving.

Since playing chess is an activity particularly challenging that requires the orchestration of various resources cognitive factors such as memory, attention and perceptual grouping: They hoped to find that the part left brain of the experts, was much more active, but not that outside the right hemisphere.

Your times reaction to simple forms were the same, but experts used both sides of your brain to respond more quickly to questions about chess positions, which means that chess activates both hemispheres cerebral.

And since the brain righ hemisphere is responsible for creativity, we won't be surprised to know that activation of the right part of the children's brain helps them develop your creative side.

In fact, since the 1960s Antonio Quiroz had said:

"Chess teaches you to use the two cerebral hemispheres".

Bertrand Russel in his book *"The Conquest of Happiness"* tells us: *"All pleasure that does not harm another person, has its own value"*. In this work, he tells us the anecdote of the great Russian writer Leon Tolstoy, whom in his years youth was awarded the Military Cross, for their behavior in the battle and when it is time to present to pick it up, I was so engrossed playing chess, he decided to give it up.

As the excellent educator that Bertrand Rusell was, warns its readers about the fact of that chess is addictive and therefore:

"It is of the utmost importance that everyone who practices it exercise it with measure".

In Mexico in January 2020, in the newspaper El Universal, journalist Javier Vargas, gave us the news: "The Kasparov Foundation for Ibero-America, chaired by the cultural promoter Hiquíngari Carranza, is driving an initiative to incorporate chess as a pedagogical strategy in the system national education".

The project includes modifications to the current General Law of Rights of Girls, Boys and Adolescents, to include chess as a subject in full-time schools. It was present by Senator Martí Batres in the Mexican Congress in order to be transferred to the respective Commission of Education and Legislative Studies. Once approved by the Senate, it will go to the Chamber of Deputies. If it ratifies it, will return to the source instance in order to that, in due course, send it to the Executive National for its final aprovment".

Printed in the United States
by Baker & Taylor Publisher Services